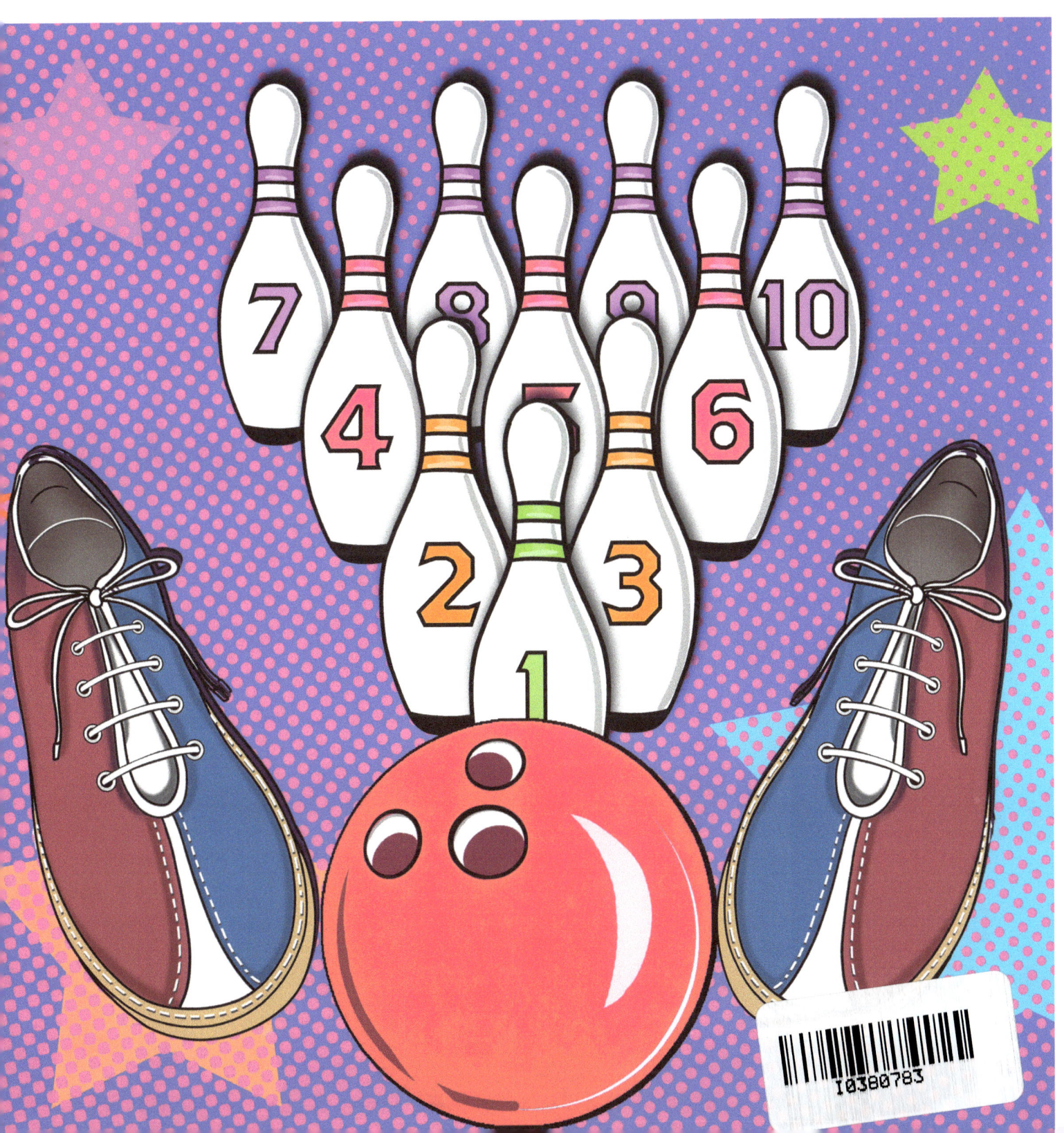

Copyright © 2021
Wayne L. Davis, Ph.D.

All rights reserved. This book or any portion thereof may not be reproduced or used in any manner whatsoever without the express written permission of the publisher except for the use of brief quotations in a book review or scholarly journal.

LoGiudice Publishing
Orland, IN 46776

Library of Congress Control Number: 2021904922

Authors:

Heather Trapp

Wayne L. Davis, Ph.D.

Illustrator:

Dawn Larder

AN INTRODUCTION TO WOMEN'S COLLEGIATE BOWLING

AUTHORS: HEATHER TRAPP & WAYNE L. DAVIS, PH.D.

ILLUSTRATIONS: DAWN LARDER

WHEN IT IS TOO COLD OUTSIDE TO RUN AROUND, GO BOWLING! BOWLING CAN BE A HARD SPORT TO UNDERSTAND, BUT HERE ARE SOME THINGS TO HELP YOU OUT.

In women's collegiate bowling, there are two different formats for how the games are played: traditional format and Baker format. In traditional bowling, each person will bowl 10 frames. In a Baker game, multiple bowlers will combine to bowl one game: bowler 1 will bowl frames 1 & 6; bowler 2 will bowl frames 2 & 7; bowler 3 will bowl frames 3 & 8; bowler 4 will bowl frames 4 & 9; and bowler 5 will bowl frames 5 & 10. In Baker games, bowler 1, who is the leadoff bowler, is the most consistent bowler and she will help the rest of the team get a good read on the lane conditions. The fifth bowler is usually the best bowler and she is expected to end the game with a turkey (i.e., three strikes).

THERE ARE 10 FRAMES IN ONE GAME. FOR EVERY FRAME, YOU CAN THROW UP TO TWO SHOTS TO KNOCK ALL OF THE PINS DOWN (EXCEPT FOR THE 10TH FRAME, WHERE YOU CAN POTENTIALLY HAVE UP TO THREE THROWS). IF YOU KNOCK ALL 10 PINS DOWN ON THE FIRST TRY, THEN THAT IS THE END OF THAT FRAME (EXCEPT FOR THE 10TH FRAME BECAUSE A STRIKE IN THE 10TH FRAME ALLOWS FOR TWO MORE THROWS).

KNOCKING ALL 10 PINS DOWN ON THE VERY FIRST TRY IN A FRAME IS CALLED A STRIKE. IF IT TAKES TWO ATTEMPTS IN A FRAME TO KNOCK ALL 10 PINS DOWN, THEN THAT IS CALLED A SPARE. IF A BOWLER OBTAINS A STRIKE IN THE 10TH FRAME, THEN THE BOWLER IS ALLOWED TWO ADDITIONAL THROWS. IF A BOWLER OBTAINS A SPARE IN THE 10TH FRAME, THEN THE BOWLER IS ALLOWED ONE ADDITIONAL THROW.

STRIKES AND SPARES ARE BOTH VERY IMPORTANT FOR GETTING A HIGH SCORE. STRIKES ARE WORTH 10 POINTS PLUS THE VALUE OF THE NEXT TWO SHOTS. SPARES ARE WORTH 10 POINTS PLUS THE VALUE OF THE NEXT ONE SHOT. THUS, GETTING A STRIKE IS BETTER THAN GETTING A SPARE.

THERE ARE 10 PINS TOTAL IN A RACK. BEFORE YOU THROW A SHOT, WE CALL ALL 10 PINS A RACK. THERE ARE FOUR ROWS OF PINS IN A 10-PIN RACK. THE FIRST ROW HAS ONE PIN, THE SECOND ROW HAS TWO PINS, THE THIRD ROW HAS THREE PINS, AND THE FOURTH ROW HAS FOUR PINS.

EVERY PIN HAS ITS OWN NUMBER. THE LONE PIN IN THE FIRST ROW CLOSET TO THE BOWLER IS CALLED THE HEADPIN, AND ITS NUMBER IS 1. READING FROM LEFT TO RIGHT, THE SECOND ROW CONTAINS PINS 2 AND 3. IN THE THIRD ROW ARE PINS 4, 5, AND 6. FINALLY, IN THE FOURTH ROW, WHICH IS FARTHEST FROM THE BOWLER, ARE PINS 7, 8, 9, AND 10.

THE HIGHEST SCORE THAT ANYONE CAN ACHIEVE IN ONE GAME OF BOWLING IS 300 POINTS. TO ACHIEVE A SCORE OF 300 POINTS IN 10 FRAMES, A BOWLER MUST OBTAIN A STRIKE ON EVERY THROW OF THE GAME FOR A TOTAL OF 12 STRIKES. THE BOWLER MUST OBTAIN A STRIKE IN EACH OF THE FIRST NINE FRAMES AND THREE STRIKES IN THE 10TH FRAME.

THERE IS NO BOWLING HANDICAP IN WOMEN'S COLLEGIATE BOWLING. A BOWLING HANDICAP PROVIDES LESS EFFECTIVE BOWLERS WITH A PREDETERMINED NUMBER OF ADDITIONAL POINTS SO THAT THEY CAN HAVE AN EQUAL CHANCE OF WINNING AGAINST BETTER BOWLERS. SIMPLY PUT, IN WOMEN'S COLLEGIATE BOWLING, THE ONLY POINTS THAT ARE USED TO DETERMINE THE WINNER ARE BASED ON THE TOTAL NUMBER OF PINS THAT ARE KNOCKED DOWN IN EACH FRAME.

THE ACTUAL NUMBER OF GAMES PLAYED DURING A WOMEN'S COLLEGIATE COMPETITION VARIES FROM TOURNAMENT TO TOURNAMENT. A SET CONTAINS THREE GAMES, AND THE SCORES FOR THE THREE GAMES WILL BE ADDED TOGETHER. THE HIGHEST SCORE FOR A SET THAT ANYONE CAN ACHIEVE IS 900 POINTS (I.E., 300 POINTS FOR EACH OF THE THREE GAME). THERE ARE ONLY A FEW PEOPLE WHO HAVE EVER DONE THIS.

There are four parts to a bowling lane: the approach, the foul line, the lane, and the pin deck. The approach, which is 15-feet long, is where the bowlers take aim at the pins and begin moving toward the pins. The approach ends at the foul line, which separates the approach from the bowling lane. The bowling lane, which is 3.5 feet wide, is the surface that the bowling balls roll on toward the pins. The pin deck is the area where the 10 bowling pins are set up.

ON EITHER SIDE OF THE BOWLING LANE IS A GUTTER, WHICH WILL CATCH A BOWLING BALL THAT DOES NOT STAY ON THE LANE. A BOWLER DOES NOT WANT TO THROW A BALL INTO A GUTTER. IF A BALL ENTERS A GUTTER, IT IS A DEAD BALL. IF THE BALL BOUNCES OUT OF THE GUTTER AND KNOCKS ANY PINS DOWN, THE FALLEN PINS WILL NOT COUNT TOWARD THE BOWLER'S SCORE. IN SHORT, IF YOU THROW YOUR BOWLING BALL INTO THE GUTTER, YOUR SCORE WILL BE A ZERO FOR THAT SHOT AND THE PINS WILL BE RESET. HOWEVER, IF YOU THROW A GUTTER BALL ON YOUR FIRST SHOT, YOU WILL STILL GET A SECOND SHOT FOR THAT FRAME.

THE PINSETTER IS A MACHINE THAT SETS BOWLING PINS BACK TO THEIR ORIGINAL POSITION, CLEARS FALLEN PINS ON THE PIN DECK, CLEARS STANDING PINS AT THE END OF A FRAME, AND SENDS THE BOWLING BALL INTO THE BOWLING BALL RETURN MECHANISM, WHICH RETURNS THE BOWLING BALL TO THE BOWLER.

SOMETIMES YOUR HANDS MAY GET WET DUE TO SWEAT, BUT WE DO HAVE SOMETHING THAT YOU CAN USE TO DRY THEM. IT IS CALLED ROSIN, WHICH COMES IN SMALL BAGS THAT YOU CAN CARRY WITH YOU. A ROSIN BAG WILL SOAK UP ANYTHING THAT CAN BE ABSORBED. YOU CAN ALSO USE THE AIR FROM THE BALL RETURN MACHINE. THERE IS A LITTLE VENT IN THE BALL RETURN MACHINE THAT BLOWS AIR, WHICH YOU CAN USE TO DRY YOUR HANDS.

THE SETTEE IS THE SEATING AREA BEHIND THE BOWLING AREA WHERE BOWLERS WAIT FOR THEIR TURN TO BOWL. THE CONCOURSE IS THE AREA BEHIND THE LANE WHERE SPECTATORS SIT TO WATCH.

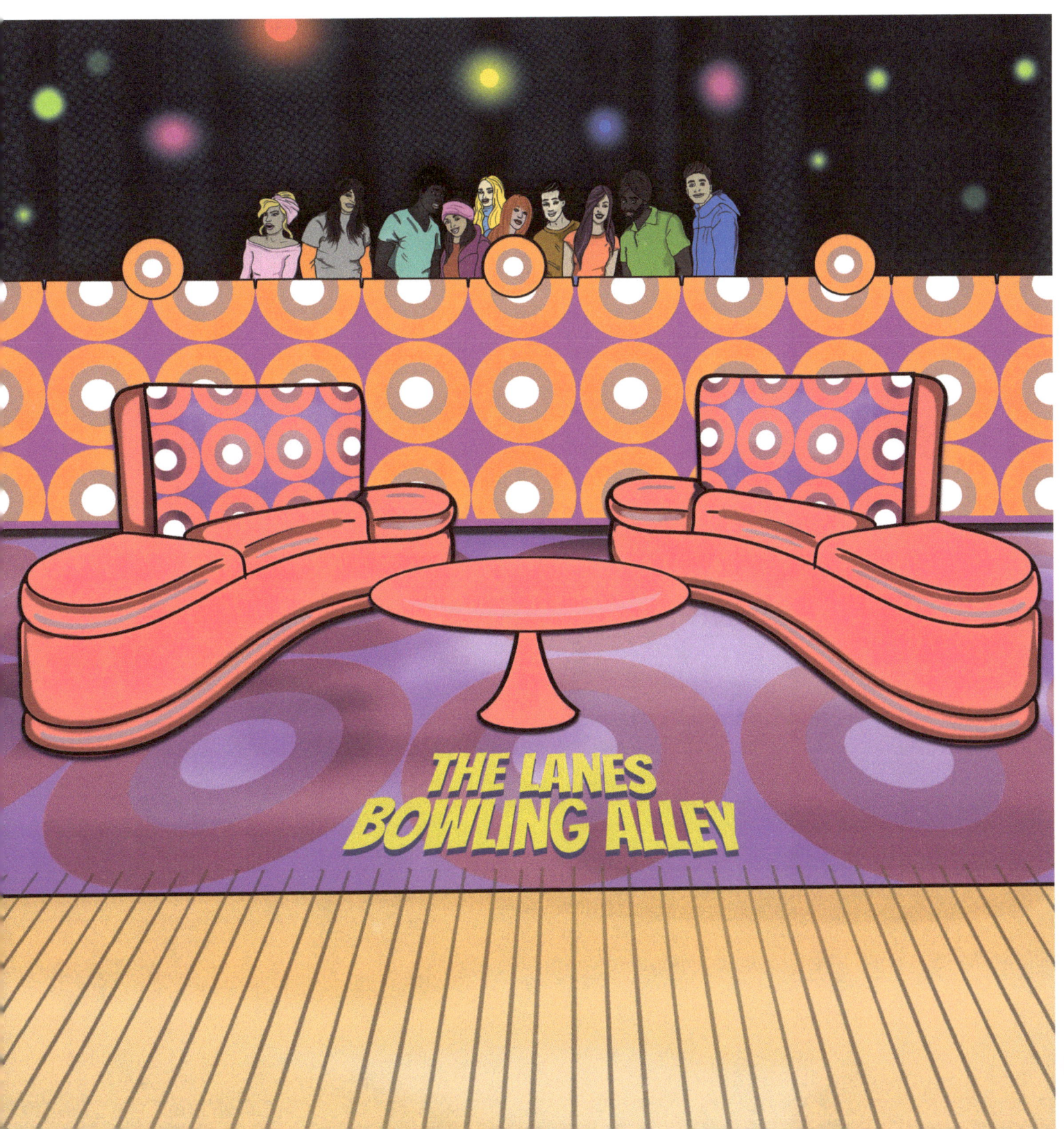

THERE ARE NO HARD RULES FOR SETTING TARGETS. BOWLERS NEED TO MATCH THEIR BOWLING STYLES TO THEIR STANCE LOCATIONS, RELEASE POSITIONS, FOCAL POINTS, LANE CONDITIONS, AND TARGETS. BOWLERS CAN USE THE DOTS AND ARROWS ON THE APPROACH AND LANE TO HELP THEM TAKE AIM AT THE TARGET PINS.

BOARDS MAKE UP THE LANE AND THE APPROACH. A BOWLING LANE HAS 39 BOARDS WITH BOARD NUMBER 20 ALWAYS BEING IN THE CENTER, WHICH IS IN ALIGNMENT WITH THE HEADPIN. FOR LEFT-HANDED BOWLERS, BOARD ONE IS THE BOARD FARTHEST TO THE LEFT. FOR RIGHT-HANDED BOWLERS, BOARD ONE IS THE BOARD FARTHEST TO THE RIGHT. BOARDS ARE USED TO HELP A BOWLER LINE UP WITH THE PINS AND TO DETERMINE THE INTENDED PATH THAT THE BALL SHOULD TAKE TOWARD THE PINS.

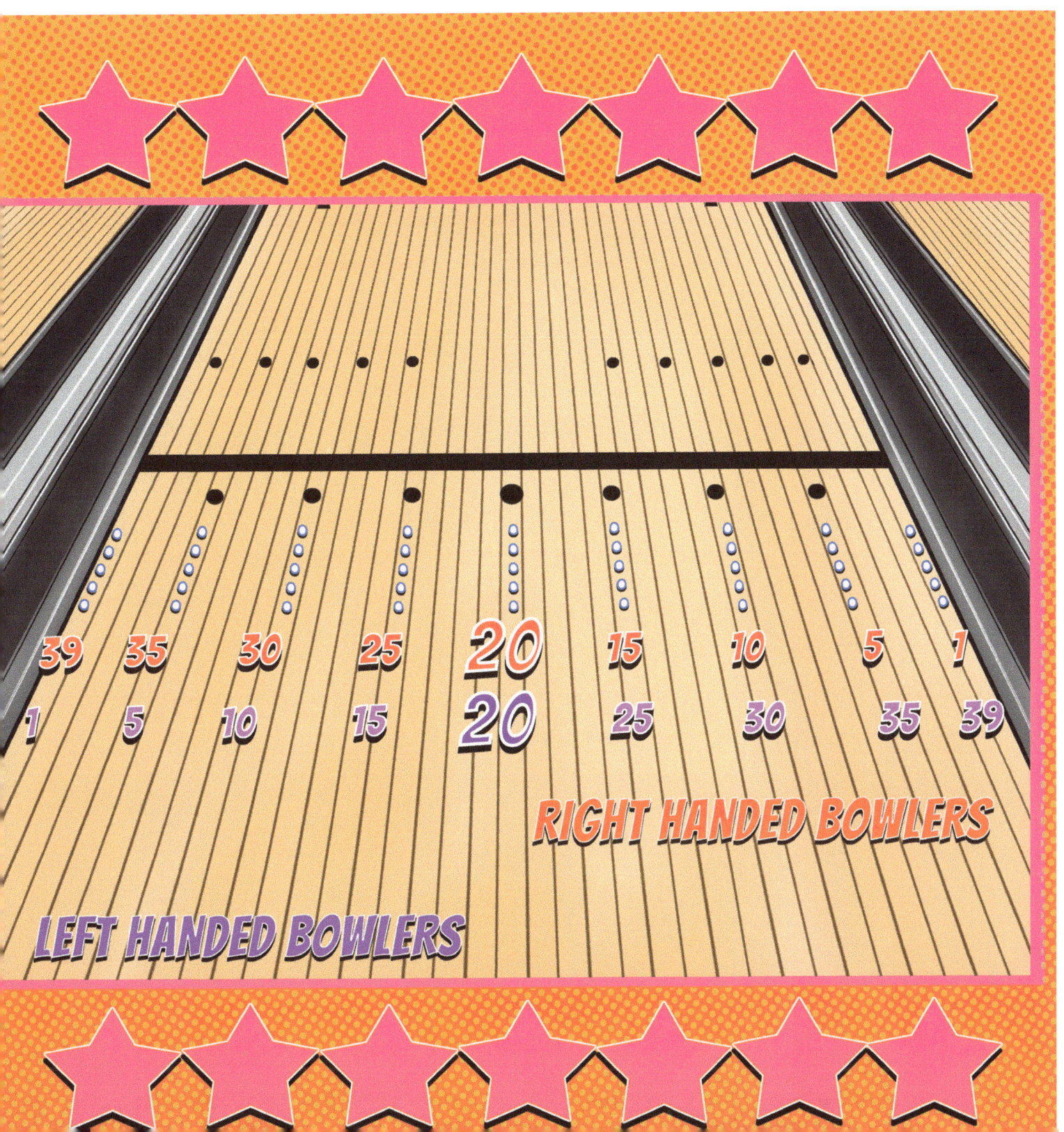

There are approach dots on every fifth board to assist bowlers in aligning their feet when they consider the direction of each throw. The dots are separated by five boards and the largest dot is on board 20, which is in alignment with the headpin. In addition, there are seven target arrows located 15 to 17 feet beyond the foul line to help bowlers provide an accurate delivery. Similar to the biggest dot on the approach, the biggest arrow on the lane is on board 20, which is in alignment with the headpin.

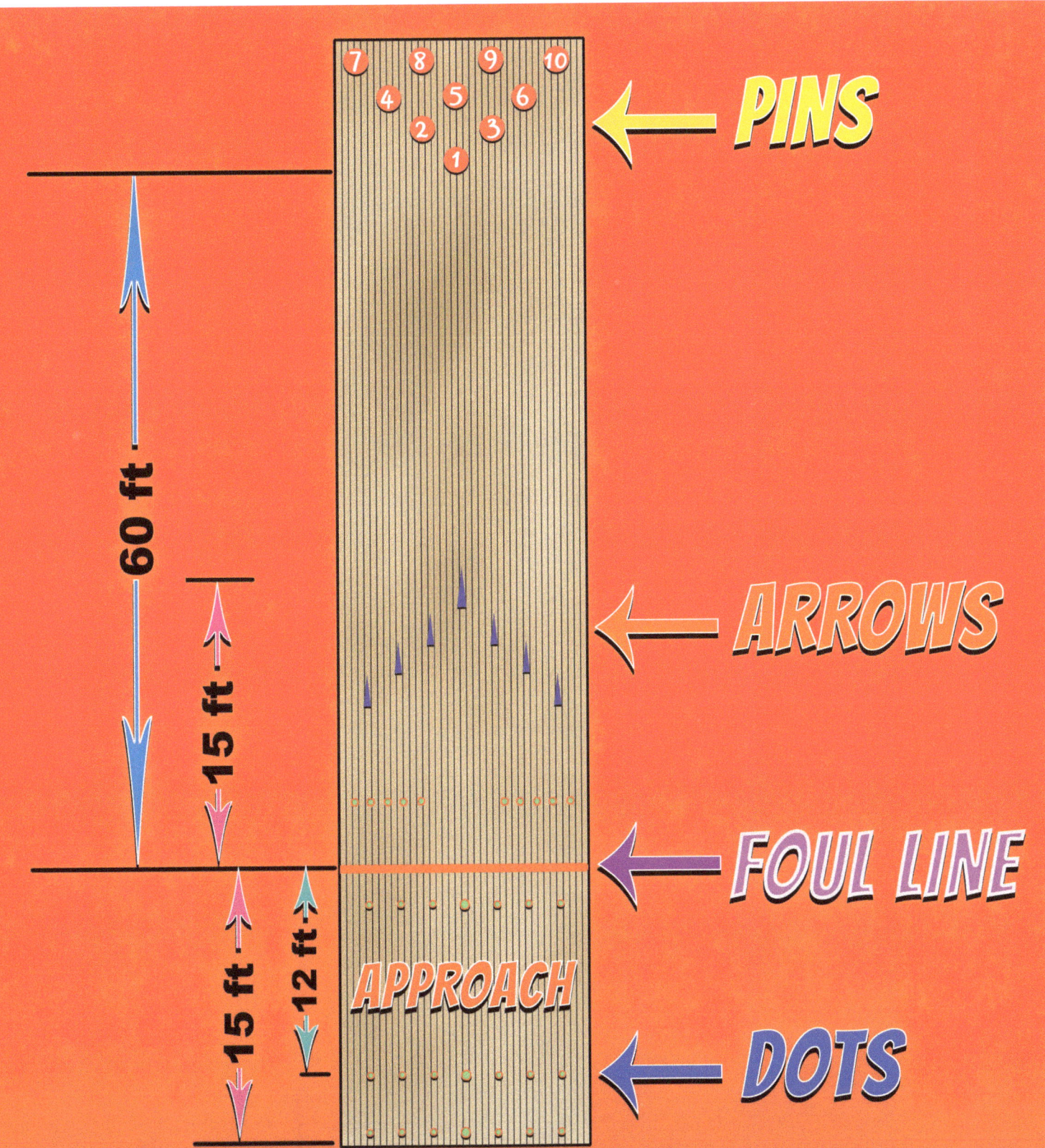

A FOUL LINE SEPARATES THE APPROACH FROM THE BOWLING LANE. THE FOUL LINE EXTENDS ACROSS THE ENTIRE BOWLING CENTER; ITS LENGTH EXTENDS INDEFINITELY AND IS NOT RESTRICTED TO JUST WHAT IS PRINTED ON THE BOARDS. IF ANY PART OF YOUR BODY, SUCH AS YOUR TOE OR HAND, GOES PAST THE FOUL LINE DURING THE RELEASE OF THE BOWLING BALL, THEN IT IS A FOUL. IF YOU PASS THE FOUL LINE BUT YOU DO NOT LET GO OF THE BOWLING BALL, THEN IT IS NOT A FOUL BECAUSE YOU DID NOT RELEASE THE BALL.

FOR A FOUL, FOOTWEAR AND CLOTHING ARE CONSIDERED PART OF YOUR BODY, BUT ACCESSORIES ARE NOT. THUS, IF YOU DROP YOUR HAT PAST THE FOUL LINE AND ONTO THE BOWLING LANE, THEN IT IS A FOUL. HOWEVER, IF YOU DROP YOUR BRACELET PAST THE FOUL LINE AND ONTO THE BOWLING LANE, IT IS NOT A FOUL. A BOWLER SHOULD REQUEST PERMISSION TO CROSS THE FOUL LINE BEFORE RETRIEVING ANY ITEMS THAT HAVE FALLEN BEYOND THE FOUL LINE AND ONTO THE BOWLING LANE.

PASSING THE FOUL LINE WILL GENERATE A LOUD NOISE AND, LIKE A GUTTER BALL, WILL RESULT IN A SCORE OF ZERO POINTS. A FOUL IS CONSIDERED A MISS AND IT WILL BE RECORDED AS AN "F" IN THE FRAME. IF IT IS THE FIRST SHOT OF THE FRAME, THEN THE PINS WILL BE RESET. HOWEVER, IF THE FOUL OCCURS ON THE SECOND SHOT, THEN THAT WILL BE THE END OF YOUR TURN FOR THAT FRAME. IN ADDITION, CROSSING THE FOUL LINE CAN BE DANGEROUS BECAUSE OIL IS PLACED ON THE LANE, WHICH CAN MAKE IT EXTREMELY SLIPPERY.

FOULING IS A MAJOR DISPUTE THAT OCCURS IN COLLEGE BOWLING. SOME FOUL ALARMS SOUND OFF WHEN THEY ARE NOT SUPPOSED TO SOUND OFF. IF THE SYSTEM INDICATES THAT YOU HAVE FOULED, BUT YOUR FOOT DID NOT CROSS THE LINE, THEN YOU MUST STAY WHERE YOU ARE AND CALL THE OFFICIAL TO COME AND LOOK. IF THE OFFICIAL SAYS THAT YOU DID NOT FOUL, THEN THE OFFICIAL WILL ADJUST THE SCORE.

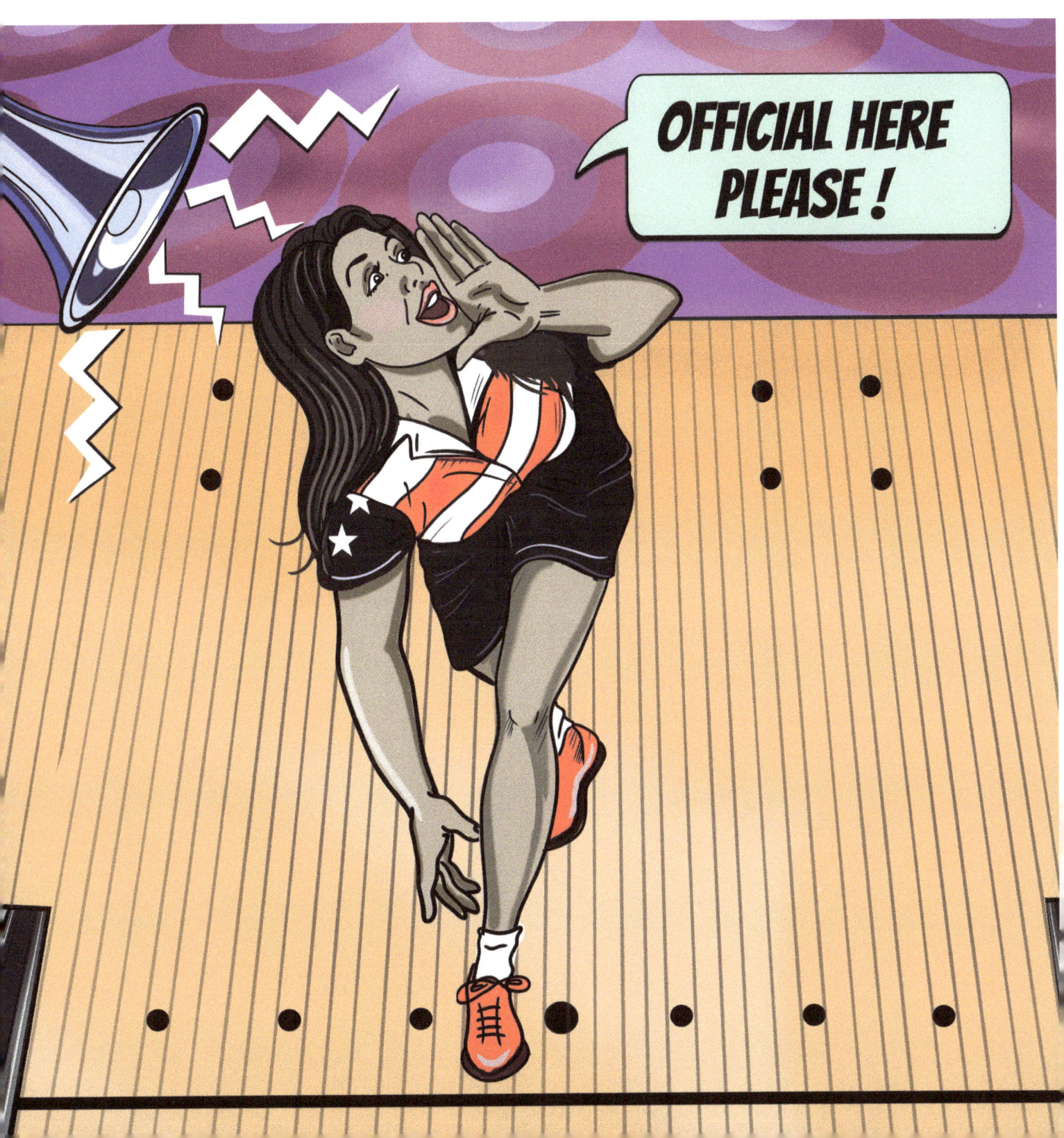

A SITUATION THAT DEMANDS THE SERVICE OF A TOURNAMENT OFFICIAL INVOLVES SCORING. IF YOU NEED A SCORE CHANGE, THEN YOU WILL NEED TO CALL THE OFFICIAL OVER TO CHANGE IT.

A BOWLING LANE IS 60 FEET LONG FROM THE FOUL LINE TO THE HEAD-PIN! THAT IS WHY WE NEED BOARDS. THE BOARDS CAN HELP A BOWLER HIT THE POCKET, WHICH IS A LONG DISTANCE AWAY.

THE POCKET FOR A RIGHT-HANDER BOWLER IS BETWEEN PINS ONE AND THREE. THE BOWLING BALL WILL CONTACT THE RIGHT SIDE OF THE HEADPIN FIRST AND THEN IT WILL CONTACT PIN THREE NEXT. THE POCKET FOR A LEFT-HANDER BOWLER IS BETWEEN PINS ONE AND TWO. THE BOWLING BALL WILL CONTACT THE LEFT SIDE OF THE HEADPIN FIRST AND THEN IT WILL CONTACT PIN TWO NEXT.

THERE ARE THREE HOLES DRILLED IN A BOWLING BALL FOR THREE DIFFERENT FINGERS. SOMETIMES, AN ADDITIONAL HOLE, WHICH IS A SMALL VENT HOLE, MAY BE DRILLED TO RELIEVE THE SUCTION IN THE HOLE USED FOR THE THUMB. THE CORRECT FINGERS TO USE IN A BOWLING BALL ARE YOUR THUMB, MIDDLE FINGER, AND RING FINGER. MOST PEOPLE USE THEIR DOMINANT HAND TO BOWL, BUT THERE ARE A FEW INDIVIDUALS WHO USE THEIR NON-DOMINANT HAND TO BOWL. TRY BOTH!

Some individuals bowl with two hands. They only place their middle and ring fingers into the ball. A bowler who uses two hands will not place her thumb into her bowling ball. She will use her other hand to help grip the ball so that she does not drop it. This is becoming a popular way to bowl.

Bowling balls come in different weights. They usually range from 6 pounds to 16 pounds. A heavier ball will transfer more of its inertia to the pins and, with more energy, you will have a better chance of knocking all the pins down. However, do not try to use a ball that is too heavy for you or you might hurt your arm.

IF YOU HAVE EVER SEEN A BOWLING BALL CURVE, IT CURVES BECAUSE THERE IS A CORE IN THE MIDDLE OF THE BALL. THE HOLES IN THE BOWLING BALL ARE DRILLED RELATIVE TO THE CORE TO MAKE THE BALL UNBALANCED SO THAT THE BALL CAN SPIN.

There are many different types of bowling balls! Some bowling balls have cores that are symmetrical, which are in equal proportion from top to bottom, and some bowling balls have cores that are asymmetrical, which are not in equal proportion from top to bottom. The motion for a ball with a symmetrical core provides a more stable and consistent motion. However, asymmetrical balls are better for lanes with heavy amounts of oil or longer oil patterns, which do not provide a lot of friction.

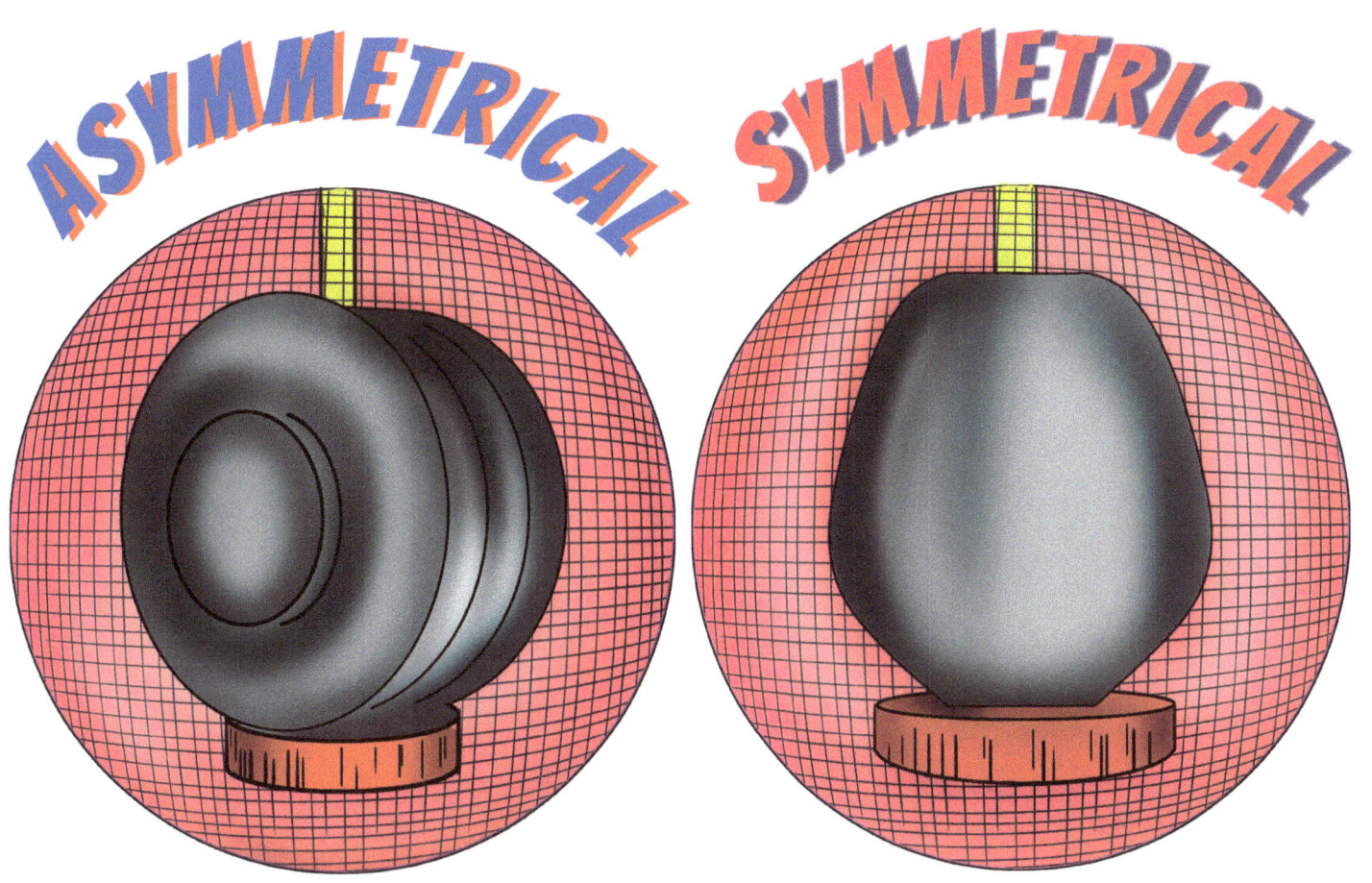

The surface of a bowling ball is usually made from one of four different types of material. We call this material the coverstock. The coverstock can be plastic, urethane, reactive resin, or particle. The coverstock is important because this is what actually makes contact with the lane surface.

YOU CAN GO TO THE LOCAL PRO SHOP TO GET YOUR BOWLING BALL DRILLED IN A MANNER THAT MATCHES YOUR BOWLING TECHNIQUE. THIS WILL ALLOW THE BALL TO WORK WITH HOW YOU THROW IT.

You can also surface your bowling ball. Surfacing is sanding the outside of your ball to create the desired amount of friction on the ball's surface. Your bowling ball will produce more friction with the lane if it has a rough surface. A ball with more friction on its surface will curve earlier than a highly polished ball.

SANDING PADS THAT ARE USED ON BOWLING BALLS CURRENTLY RANGE FROM 180 TO 4,000 GRITS. A LOWER GRIT NUMBER MEANS A ROUGHER SURFACE. IF A BOWLING LANE HAS A LOT OF OIL ON IT, A PAD WITH A LOWER GRIT NUMBER WILL BE NEEDED TO SAND THE BOWLING BALL'S SURFACE TO GET THE BALL TO BETTER CURVE. HOWEVER, DEPENDING ON CONDITIONS, IT IS POSSIBLE THAT SANDED BALLS CAN ACTUALLY CURVE LESS THAN POLISHED BALLS BECAUSE SANDED BALLS CAN LOSE TOO MUCH ENERGY TOO QUICKLY.

You can polish your bowling ball with compounds, gel polishes, and polishes that contain slip agents. A more polished and slippery bowling ball will have less friction, allowing it to conserve energy. Compared to sanded bowling balls, polished bowling balls skid farther along the bowling lane and they are best used in drier lane conditions.

IN ADDITION TO SANDING AND POLISHING, INDIVIDUALS CAN ALSO USE BALL CLEANERS. A BALL CLEANER SPINS THE BALL AND CLEANS OFF THE OIL, DIRT, SCUFF MARKS, AND BELT MARKS THAT ARE ON THE SURFACE OF YOUR BOWLING BALL.

IT IS A LOT EASIER TO CLEAN OR TO SAND THE BOWLING BALL'S SURFACE WITH THE HELP OF A BALL SPINNER. A BALL SPINNER IS A MACHINE THAT YOU PUT YOUR BOWLING BALL INTO, YOU FLIP A SWITCH, AND IT SPINS YOUR BALL. THIS MACHINE WILL ALLOW YOU TO POLISH OR SAND THE BALL'S SURFACE MORE QUICKLY THAN DOING IT MANUALLY.

During competitions, the home coach or the official will be the one who selects the oil patterns to be used on the bowling lanes. Many different patterns may be used with various amounts of oil in various locations. Some examples of shapes include a top hat, a Christmas tree, the Eiffel Tower, the Tower of Pisa, and the Statue of Liberty. In a women's collegiate bowling tournament, the same pattern, once selected, will be used on the different lanes.

Areas on the bowling lane that have less oil will cause the ball to hook more, while areas that have more oil will cause the ball to slip and slide more. During practice, for example, the bowlers learn to determine the shape of the pattern by watching the movement of the ball as it rolls down the lane. During a game, bowlers will push the oil, which will affect the action of the ball and the performance of other bowlers.

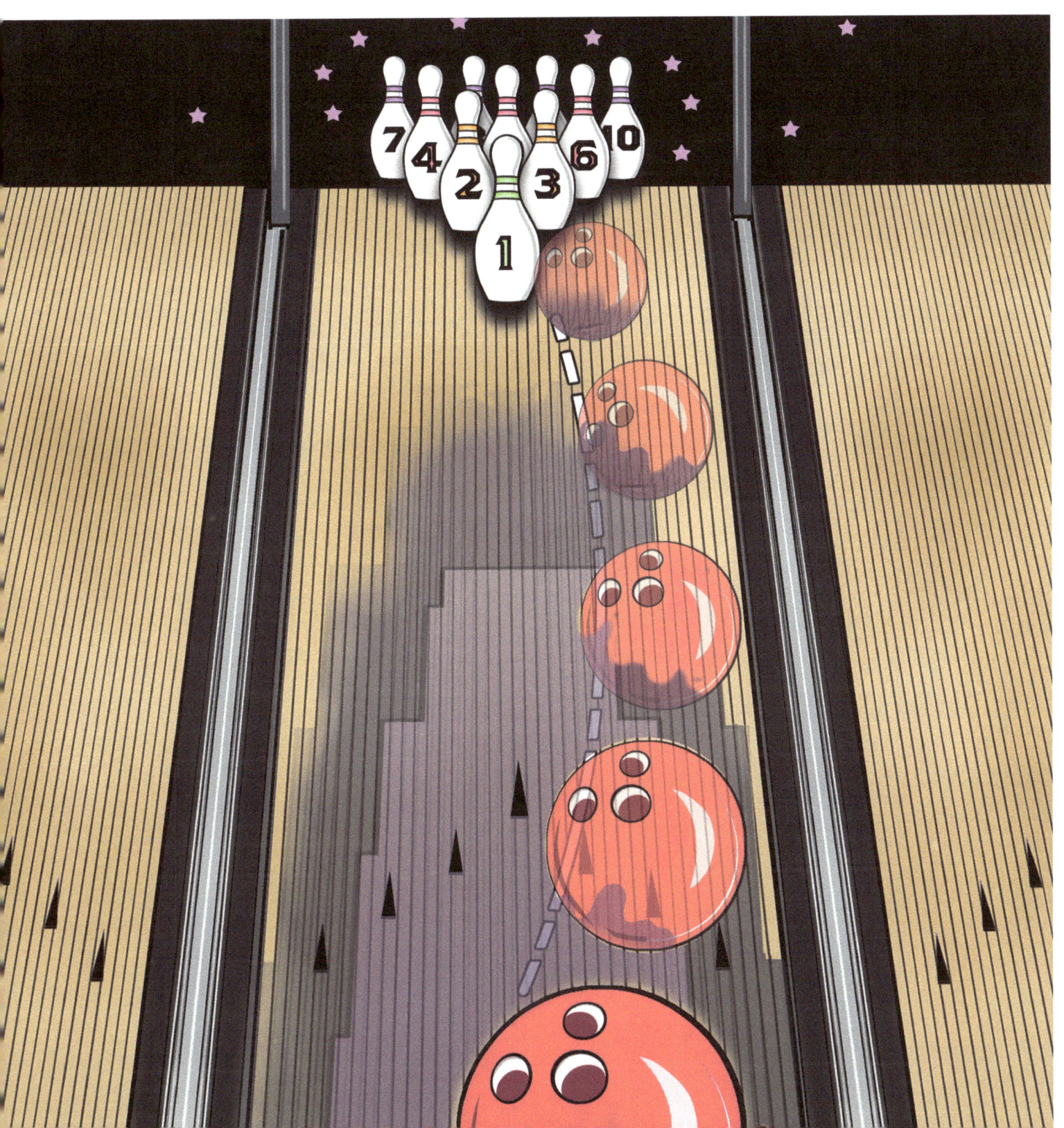

NO TWO ROLLS ON AN OIL PATTERN ARE EXACTLY THE SAME. THE BALL WILL PICK UP OIL EVERY SINGLE TIME THAT IT ROLLS DOWN THE LANE, WHICH IS TAKING IT OFF THE LANE ITSELF. IN OTHER WORDS, THERE IS AN INVERSE RELATIONSHIP BETWEEN THE NUMBER OF TIMES A BOWLING BALL ROLLS OVER A SPOT AND THE AMOUNT OF OIL AT THAT SPOT.

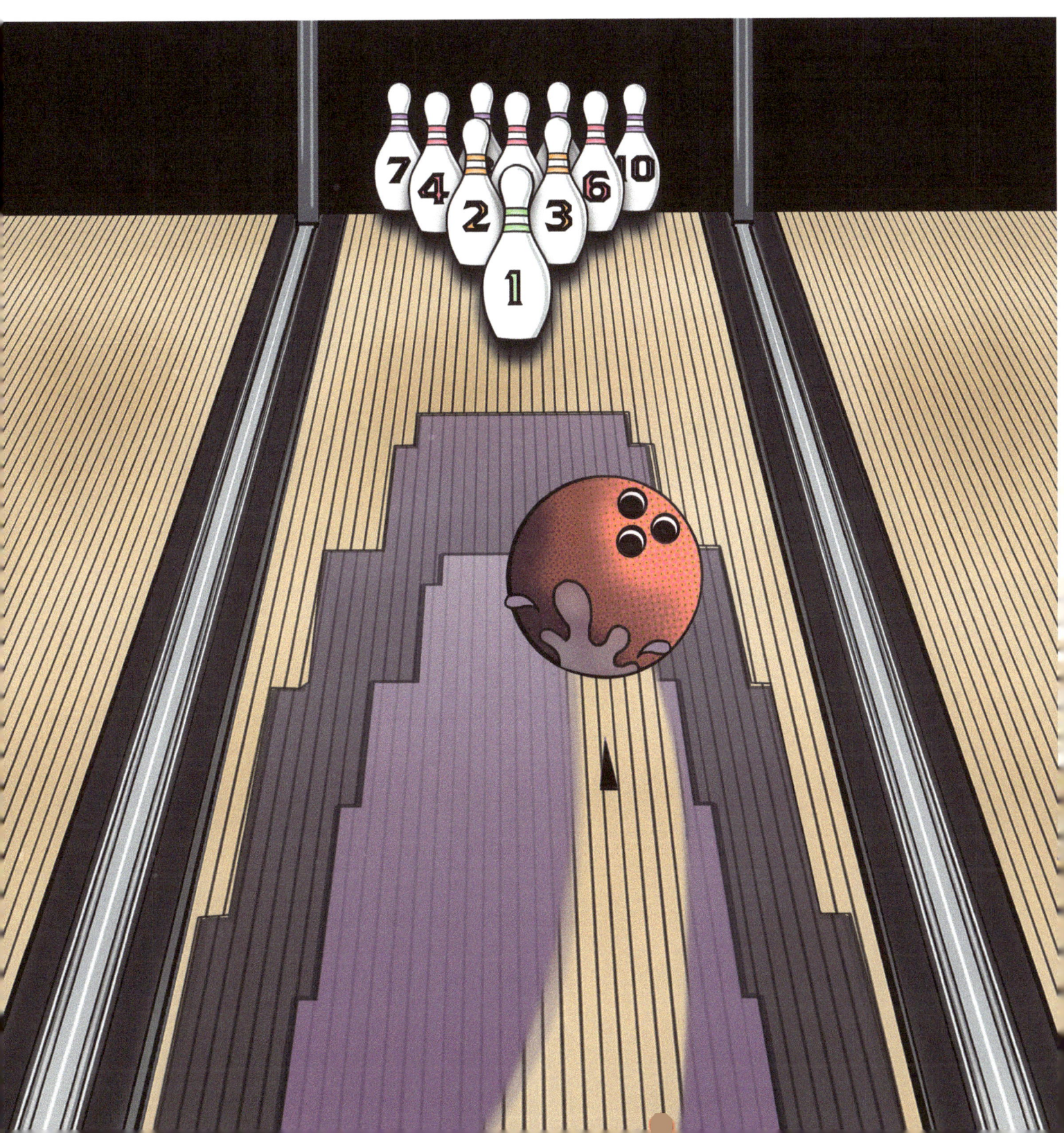

As the amount of oil changes on the lane, individuals will need to compensate for the lane's action. Bowlers will adjust the position of their feet by using the dots on the approach, and they may need to use different arrows on the lane for targeting.

BOWLING SHOES ARE ALSO VERY IMPORTANT. PEOPLE WHO ARE SERIOUS ABOUT THE SPORT OF BOWLING HAVE THEIR OWN SHOES. MOST BOWLING SHOES COME WITH SOLES AND HEELS THAT YOU CAN TAKE OFF AND SWAP WITH DIFFERENT ONES, WHICH WILL MODIFY THE LENGTH OF YOUR SLIDE. MODIFICATIONS ARE VERY IMPORTANT BECAUSE NOT EVERY APPROACH IN EVERY BOWLING ALLEY HAS THE SAME AMOUNT OF FRICTION.

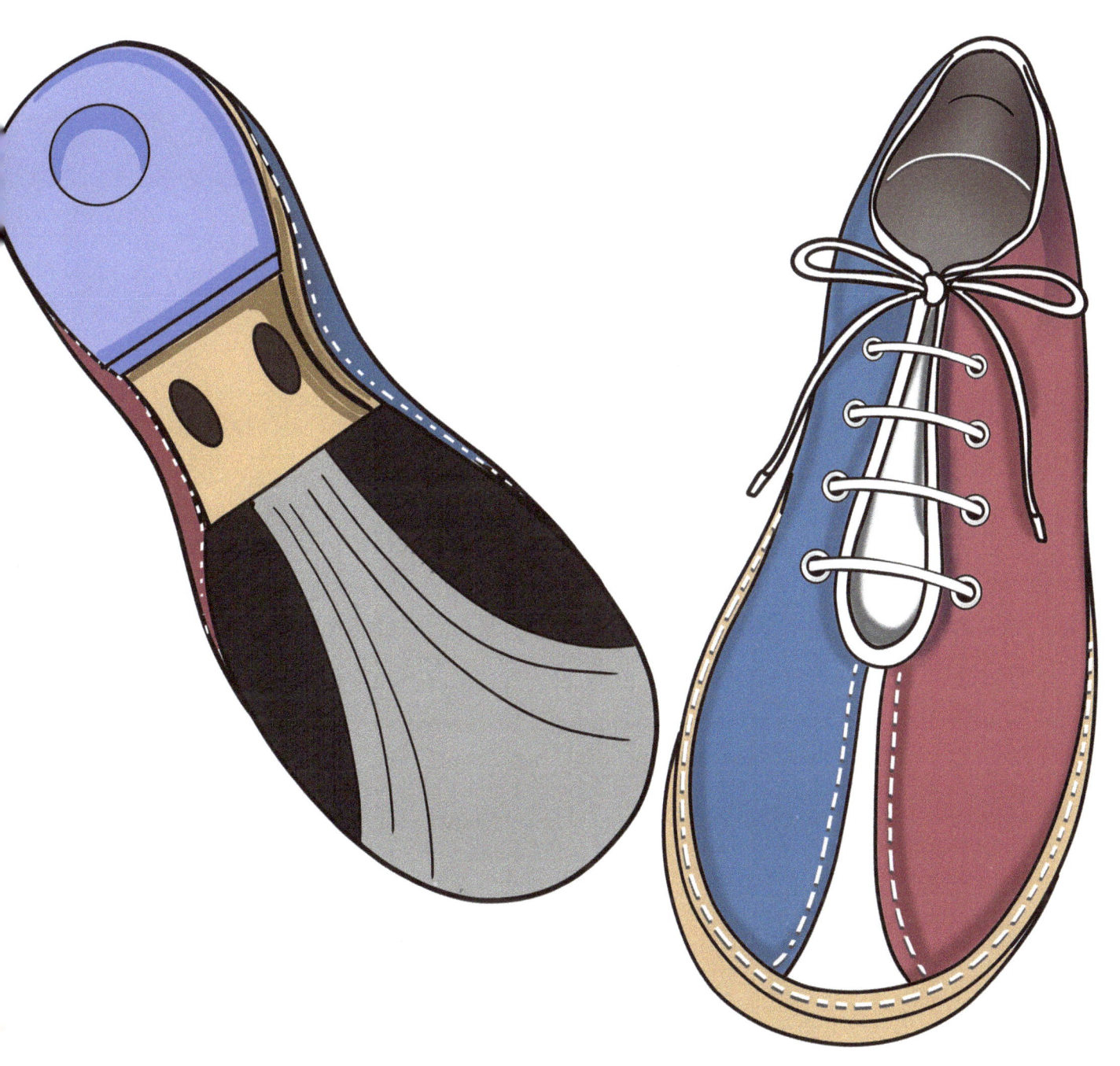

THERE ARE DIFFERENT TYPES OF SOLES AND HEELS THAT WILL ALLOW YOU TO MODIFY YOUR AMOUNT OF SLIDE. FOR EXAMPLE, THERE ARE SLIDING SOLES AND BRAKING SOLES; THERE ARE LEATHER HEELS AND RUBBER HEELS. THIS IS VERY IMPORTANT TO KNOW BECAUSE IF YOU ARE SLIDING TOO MUCH, YOU CAN SWAP YOUR SOLES OR HEELS TO ACHIEVE THE PERFECT SLIDE FOR YOUR APPROACH.

WITH ALL THE PRESSURE THAT YOU PUT ON YOUR SHOES EVERY TIME THAT YOU BOWL, THE SOLE WILL EVENTUALLY FLATTEN, WHICH WILL CREATE MORE FRICTION AND WILL REDUCE THE AMOUNT OF SLIDE ON THE APPROACH. THIS COULD BE PROBLEMATIC IF YOUR SHOES STICK ON THE APPROACH AND YOU FALL FLAT ON YOUR FACE IN THE LANE, WHICH IS COVERED IN OIL.

SHOE BRUSHES ARE IMPORTANT BECAUSE THEY CAN CHANGE THE AMOUNT OF FRICTION ON THE SOLE. SHOE BRUSHES LOOK LIKE LITTLE WIRE BRUSHES. THE BOWLER CAN BRUSH THE BOTTOM OF THE SHOE FROM HEEL TO TOE, FROM TOE TO HEEL, OR FROM SIDE TO SIDE TO ADJUST THE AMOUNT OF SLIDE.

Sometimes, a bowler may not want to slide during her release and, therefore, she will plant her sliding foot. We call this planting. She will wear shoes that help reduce the amount of slide. However, planting can create a lot of stress on the knee.

SPARE BALLS ARE BOWLING BALLS THAT ARE MADE OF PLASTIC. THEY ARE DESIGNED TO ROLL STRAIGHT AND NOT TO BE AFFECTED BY THE OIL PATTERN ON THE LANE. THEY ARE EFFECTIVE FOR SPARE SHOTS WITH SINGLE PINS. A SINGLE PIN IS A BOWLING PIN THAT IS STANDING ALONE WITH NO OTHER BOWLING PINS IN THE PIN DECK AREA.

ONE OF THE MOST DIFFICULT SPLITS TO PICK UP IS THE 7-10 SPLIT (I.E., THE 7 PIN AND THE 10 PIN). BY DEFINITION, SPLIT PINS ARE NOT ADJACENT TO ONE ANOTHER AND THEY HAVE A GAP (I.E., A MISSING PIN) BETWEEN THEM.

There are all kinds of ways to walk on the approach. Some individuals take three steps, some take four, and some take five. Some individuals even take more! Women collegiate bowlers who are serious about bowling will take either four or five steps. You should be balanced and comfortable during the steps.

THERE ARE COACHES IN WOMEN'S COLLEGIATE BOWLING. THEY HELP GET EVERYTHING SET UP FOR TOURNAMENTS AND THEY COME UP WITH PRACTICE SCHEDULES. THEY HELP ALL TEAM BOWLERS GET BETTER THROUGHOUT THEIR COLLEGE CAREERS.

There is no rule that sets a maximum number of bowlers for a women's collegiate bowling team. However, the minimum number of bowlers on a team is five bowlers.

A WOMEN'S COLLEGIATE BOWLING TEAM MAY HAVE A CAPTAIN, BUT IT IS AT THE COACH'S PLEASURE. FOR EXAMPLE, A COACH MAY BELIEVE THAT ALL TEAM MEMBERS SHOULD BE EQUALLY INVOLVED AND, THEREFORE, THE COACH MAY REFUSE TO DESIGNATE A TEAM CAPTAIN.

There is etiquette, or a set of unwritten rules, in bowling. First, you should not wear street shoes when bowling because they can transfer dirt onto the surface of the approach. Second, you should not eat or drink in the bowling area. Third, when two people are in adjacent lanes, the first person on the approach will go first: when in doubt, the bowler on the right, when facing the pins, will go first. Fourth, you should keep any post-shot celebration or display of anger in your own bowling area: you should not encroach upon the areas of other bowlers. Fifth, you should be ready to bowl when it is your turn. Sixth, you should not linger on the approach. Finally, you should be respectful of your opponents.

THERE ARE TWO NATIONAL CHAMPIONSHIPS FOR WOMEN'S COLLEGIATE BOWLING: UNITED STATES BOWLING CONGRESS (USBC) OPEN CHAMPIONSHIPS AND THE NATIONAL COLLEGIATE ATHLETIC ASSOCIATION (NCAA) CHAMPIONSHIPS. IT IS POSSIBLE COMPETE IN BOTH NATIONAL CHAMPIONSHIPS.

PRACTICE, PRACTICE, PRACTICE! THE ONLY WAY TO GET BETTER AT BOWLING IS TO PRACTICE! FIND A LEAGUE NEAR YOU AND BOWL A FEW TIMES A WEEK. THIS IS A GROWING SPORT AND THERE ARE MANY OPPORTUNITIES OUT THERE FOR YOU! MOST IMPORTANTLY, HAVE FUN DOING IT.

HEATHER TRAPP BOWLS FOR LINCOLN MEMORIAL UNIVERSITY IN HARROGATE, TENNESSEE. SHE WAS THE TEAM'S VERY FIRST BOWLER, SO HER COLLEGIATE NUMBER IS 01. HEATHER HAS BEEN BOWLING FOR OVER 15 YEARS!

DR. WAYNE L. DAVIS TEACHES GRADUATE AND UNDERGRADUATE CRIMINAL JUSTICE COURSES AT LINCOLN MEMORIAL UNIVERSITY. HE ENJOYS INVESTIGATING THE TECHNIQUES, STRATEGIES, AND ISSUES OF THE GAME.